Touched
by the Hand of
God

In the City of Angels

SEND ME!

Patricia L. Blake

Library of Congress Control Number: 2024911843

ISBN: 979-8-89419-494-3 (sc)
ISBN: 979-8-89419-495-0 (hc)
ISBN: 979-8-89419-496-7 (e)

THE EWINGS PUBLISHING

One Galleria Blvd., Suite 1900, Metairie, LA 70001
(504) 702-6708

Touched
by the Hand of
God

In the City of Angels

SEND ME!

Patricia L. Blake

CONTENTS

INTRODUCTION

Faith, Angels, Warriors, and Evil— SEND ME!

The following firsthand experiences of over thirty-three years of police work hopefully provide insight into the human side of everyday law enforcement officers, their daily emotions, and challenges. There are personal and factual accounts of childhood years through a proud career in police service reflecting a common thread of deep spiritual faith. For the majority of officers throughout the nation, law enforcement is more than a job – it is a true Calling to protect the innocent, the vulnerable, and the helpless. These officers possess the instinct to run into danger without hesitation. Thank God for his guardian angels watching over our brothers and sisters in Blue.

The adventure begins with a brief history of the Los Angeles Police Department. You are presented with the culture of what it takes to become a police officer. The selection process to become a police officer begins with the application process, academy training, and probation. Many do not make the cut. Day one at the police academy is an eye-opener. From this moment onward, the candidate and their families begin to live the cost of choosing "to protect and to serve" our community. The personal adventures described are real-life experiences that my brothers and sisters in Blue and I lived. This personal testimony provides insight into the real world sacrifices and challenges of serving as a police officer are on a daily basis, as well as the impact on their families and children. I did not seek to embellish, glamorize, or dramatize police officers. I will leave that to Hollywood. There is already enough entertainment focused action TV series and movies. Most inaccurately portray police work for sheer action and entertainment value.

My intent is different. Hopefully, you will be entertained, but my focus is to document factual personal accounts of what it is like to be a police officer. The unfolding true events included in this book will open a window for you on bringing to life the dangerous, tragic, and unpredictable side of street police work. Join me as I describe Los Angeles police officers and their partners during daily patrol on the streets of Los Angeles.

Ride "shotgun" as you respond Code Three in a black-and-white patrol vehicle, lights and sirens activated; respond to "shots fired" calls, "officer needs help" radio broadcasts, grand theft auto chases of suspects in tense vehicle pursuits; and confront dangerous combative suspects. Be ready for an emotional ride with field officers, live the LAPD motto "To Protect and to Serve." Set up perimeters, contain, chase, and apprehend the suspect. Live the Calling to "get the bad guy," ideally without injury to the suspect, victims, or the officers. Join the excitement responding to and handling life and death radio calls.

Personally witness the grief and emotional impact of tragic incidents no person should have to see, forever imprinted in memory no matter how hard you try to forget.

This writing honors all our brave police, fire, and medical first responders on the domestic front as well as our brave military personnel on the front lines. They are true warriors and protectors who courageously and honorably risk their lives on a daily basis in the line of duty; without hesitation, these true heroes are willing to make the ultimate sacrifice for a total stranger. These warriors are blessed by God, who sends guardian angels to watch over, shield, and protect them. God also calls on our first responders in the form of guardian angels to shield, protect, and rescue victims in their darkest moments of terror, desperation, and need.

For anyone who questions this belief and faith, carefully consider America's most catastrophic disaster of the 911 terrorist attacks on the New York City World Trade Center Twin Towers. This tragedy reflects immeasurable and repeated acts of bravery, heroism, and courage on the part of countless police and fire first responders, as well as countless courageous citizens in the face of unimaginable terror, despair, and pure evil.

Isaiah is thought of as the greatest Old Testament prophet. The Bible quotes in the book of Isaiah 6:8, *"Then I [Isaiah] heard the voice of the Lord saying, Whom shall I send? And who will go for us? And I said, 'Here am I. Send me!'"*

Isaiah was God's messenger, given God's challenging task of telling his people horrible news from God. When God calls upon us and asks, *"Whom shall I send? And who will go for us?"* The majority of our first responder warriors respond without hesitation - "SEND ME!"

This writing is dedicated to all the sworn and civilian personnel I have had the honor to have worked side by side with as partners, leaders, and mentors. These sworn, volunteer and civilian personnel are just a few of the individuals who truly make a difference each and every day throughout the nation and the world.

This endeavor could not have been completed without the support of my family, especially:

My parents, Leroy and Lorraine Blake;
My son John and daughter Jessica Lorraine
Brother Mike and sister Judy;

Grandchildren
Amber Lynn (medical field)
John (San Antonio PD)
Jeff (San Antonio PD)
Madison (Air Force, medical field)

A SPECIAL DEDICATION TO THE MEMORY OF
MOCHA LATTE, MY ANGEL WARRIOR HORSE

CHAPTER 1

This Is the City — Los Angeles

The Los Angeles Police Department (LAPD) is the third largest law enforcement agency in the nation, with New York and Chicago in the top two spots. In the year 2023, the number of sworn officers dropped from 10,000 to 8,967 officers, and 3,000 nonsworn support personnel, with a loss of over 45 officers for each of the 21 divisions citywide. LAPD is responsible for the public safety of a civilian population of approximately four million; monitors the homeless shelters along with increasing numbers of immigrants across the open border; has the largest harbor and port system on the west coast; and is responsible for the MTA line throughout the city.

Jack Webb produced *Dragnet* and *Adam-12* from 1950 to 1970. These shows depicted police work in the city of Los Angeles and made a significant childhood impression on me. These shows inspired me with a drive to protect and help others. Jack Web and Officers Malloy and Reed were my childhood heroes.

In the early 1950s, the *Dragnet* TV show made a profound and lasting public impact on the image of LAPD. Jack Webb produced and played the part of Sergeant Joe Friday, assigned as a detective in Los Angeles. The *Dragnet* TV show ran from 1951 to 1959 with partner, Officer Frank Smith (Ben Alexander). The show was brought back in 1967 with Jack Webb and his crime-solving partner, Officer Bill Gannon (Harry Morgan). The police term *dragnet* meant "a system of coordinated measures for apprehending criminals or suspects."

Jack Webb usually opened his TV show with the infamous words, *"The story you are about to see is true, the names have been changed to protect the innocent - This is the City (Los Angeles)."*

Detective Webb's LAPD issued sergeant badge stamped with the number 714 was portrayed in the backdrop. A black-and-white shot of downtown City of Los Angeles or other parts of the city filled the TV screen to set the story.

Jack Webb's police persona is infamous with his methodical, straightforward but passionate approach - best reflected in his statement to a witness during an interview, *"Just the facts ma'am,"* is fondly branded into every viewer's memory.

Jack Webb later produced the *Adam-12* series, which portrays realistic police work with a human perspective of the emotions and stress of the job. Officer Pete Malloy (Martin Milner) and rookie Officer Jim Reed (Kent McCord) handled radio calls on the streets of Los Angeles. Malloy and Reed were assigned to radio car unit "One Adam-12." (Designation "one" represents Central Area, Adam is a two-officer field patrol unit, and a section of the Area). Each primary unit took pride in handling their assigned area, called 'Area Integrity'.

Jack Webb, although never a police officer, possessed a passion for law enforcement officers and the community members. Jack Webb had a profound impact on the image of LAPD and law enforcement. He illustrated and captured the challenges of police work and human tragedy in a real sense - the capacity for human evil, the long hours and shift work, working weekends, endless paperwork, and the impact on officers' personal family lives.

His heartfelt support and respect for police officers shines through in a black and white tape of *Adam-12*, "What is a cop? Famous Speech for the Big Interrogation." Jack Webb mentors rookie Jim Reed regarding a breakup with his girlfriend because she felt police work was not good enough for their relationship. After an in-depth three-minute description about all the negative downside to the job, Webb's heartfelt and deeply moving pride for Los Angeles police work shines through:

"There are over five thousand men in this city who know that being a policeman is an endless, glamourless, thankless job that has got to be done. I know it too . . . and I'm damn glad to be one of them."

Jack Webb joined Johnny Carson to collaborate on a classic comedy skit. This unforgettable theft investigation spoof was titled the "Copper Clapper Caper." It is worthwhile to listen to the nostalgic video tapes, "What is a cop" speech and the classic "Clapper Caper" spoof. This skit highlights the subtleties, comedian, and facial nuances of two great actors and comedians.

He produced his police drama episodes using factual interviews with real police officers and actual police case files, all with minimal street violence. These two TV series were a realistic and accurate depiction of police officers daily shift work in the field. Jack Webb forever changed public perception of police work across the nation.

Note: Information obtained from the Internet, Jack Webb, Dragnet, and Adam-12.

CHAPTER 2

The Challenges of Female Officers in LAPD History

A brief history of women with the Los Angeles Police Department is provided to gain an appreciation of the unique challenges and adversity they faced to be accepted as equals with their male counterparts within the Department. Our sisters in Blue that came before us were true trailblazers within the Los Angeles Police Department.

In 1909, Alice Stebbins Wells was the first female policewoman, generally known as matrons or workers in Los Angeles with arrest powers. However, female personnel were not classified as police officers. In fact, the LAPD badges had the word "Policeman" imprinted on their Department-issued badge, and policewomen had the word "Policewoman" imprinted on their Department-issued badge. Prior to 1973, LAPD had two separate gender-based job classifications. Men in the policeman classification performed police field assignments and could be promoted to all ranks. Policewomen did not work regular field assignments of their male counterparts, instead performing tasks related to women and children, desk duty, and administration. They were barred from promotion above the level of sergeant. Policewomen carried their gun in their purse and were issued a formal hat, skirt, jacket, and blouse uniform.

In 1973, LAPD abandoned the sex segregated job classifications, forming a single-entry level position of police officer, with the words "Police Officer" stamped on their Department-issues badge.

In 1971, then LAPD Chief Ed Davis openly expressed his feeling toward female officers at a meeting with females present. Chief Davis bluntly proclaimed, "Real police work should be done by men," and females biggest drawback was that "they have monthlies."

Chief Davis's comment created a firestorm that reformed the Department forever. LAPD policewoman Fanchon Blake (no relation to this writer) with almost twenty years of service, was present at the meeting. She was furious with the chief's callous remark.

This was the trigger that started the war. Fanchon Blake took on the entire LAPD organization by initiating a class-action lawsuit against the City of Los Angeles, alleging discrimination in the department's selection, hiring, and promotional work practices for females and minorities.

It took almost eight years for the class-action lawsuit to be settled and enforced by a court order in 1981; resulting in changes in the unfair selection and recruitment, training, appointment, and performance for women and minorities in LAPD.

The Los Angeles Times described these changes in the organization as "shattering LAPD's glass ceiling for women." When the lawsuit went into effect to be enforced in 1981, there were approximately 175 females in LAPD. By the year 2010 there were almost two thousand female officers. Los Angeles Times editor David Colker wrote that Fanchon Blake's class action lawsuit "targeting the LAPD resulted in one of the most sweeping changes in the Department's history." Fanchon Blake later authored a book documenting her experiences, called "Busting the Brass Ceiling."

There was a plethora of unsubstantiated horror stories about female officers floating throughout the Department during the time increasing numbers of females began to join the Department in 1981. One rumor spread like wildfire regarding a female officer in the infamous rough Southend Watts projects. Her male partner engaged in a physical fight with a combative suspect who was overpowering the officer. The female officer allegedly panicked and ran back to the parked police vehicle and locked the vehicle doors.

Another rumor related to a female officer in Northeast Division. The female officer and her partner were breaking up a party with complaints of loud noises. The female officer reportedly shot a suspect after he ripped off her uniform tie and clip. These stories fueled the "old-timer" officers' narrative and perception that female officers on the job could not be trusted in physical field situations with combative suspects.

I looked forward to the unique challenges of serving the community to make a true difference and focused on excelling every day to prove females could do the job as equals with our male counterparts. All police officers are human regardless of gender, and we all make mistakes. All new officers and probationers have a learning curve in this complex occupation. Police street work is unpredictable and fluid, requiring reliance on ongoing training, quick assessment and decision-making in life-and-death situations, and identification of all available resources.

For those of us that joined the Department in the early 1980s, the majority of the LAPD police officer counterparts had never worked with female officers in the field and not everyone embraced the concept with open arms. Meaningful internal cultural change takes time to implement and to gain ownership on the part of the stakeholders (i.e., the sworn officers and community members) within any organization.

To our present and future sisters in Blue, never forget the struggle and obstacles our groundbreaking female officers in Blue faced with steadfast courage, tenacity, and perseverance.

These courageous female officers stood up and fought back to prove beyond a doubt that females can do the same job as their male counterparts as equals in the field - including handling fluid dangerous situations.

Note: Some information obtained from the Internet, History of LAPD Policewomen, and Fanchon Blake.

CHAPTER 3

Rowdy Childhood

A brief look of childhood days that influenced my intense sense of justice and the calling to protect the innocent and vulnerable is presented below.

The family consisted of traditional "old school" parents in the late 1950s and 1960s. We lived outside The Dalles, Oregon, near the Columbia River. Dad was an intimidating towering man at six foot, four inches and 240 pounds. He was a construction worker on the Grand Coulee Dam on the Columbia River, and a military World War II army war veteran who fought on the Pacific Islands, a brutal combat field. A grenade killed the men around him in a trench. He was in a coma for three months in Hawaii. Until the day he died, Dad had pieces of metal shrapnel surface on his arms, back, and upper body. He never complained about any pain and would pull out the metal fragments and throw them on the floor without saying a word. He was a huge fan of John Wayne but could not watch any war movies on TV and never talked about the war. He was a true war hero to our family members.

As the oldest child, my father expected me to protect and watch over my younger brother and two sisters. Dad stressed to my brother he was not allowed to hit the girls. Several times my brother was taken out to the woodshed for punishment. Dad later made an exception to that rule with me.

At the age of five, the youngest baby sister bit me on the arm, leaving teeth marks and blood. Dad was nearby and ordered me to bite her back. Instinctively feeling it unjust to bite the baby, I refused the order. The consequences were immediate, being thrown and kicked up the stairwell; and Dad bit the baby to solidify the lesson.

On various occasions, I fled on foot in fear of imminent death with my father chasing me around the outside of the house. Each time was an amazement to be able to outrun him and escape on foot to find sanctuary in the cherry orchard behind the house. Of course, victory was always brief, there were always consequences waiting for me when returning home.

When my sister fell off the hood of the car because my brother teased her with an earth worm (which I felt was more than a slight overreaction); Dad's first statement to me was, "Why did you let your sister break her arm?"

Our grandparents lived nearby in Rufus, Oregon. We loved to visit their 140 acres plus wheat farm, which included Grandpa's prized stallion and a team of plow horses to work the wheat fields. At the age of four, Grandpa sent me under the chicken coop to gather eggs. Grandpa pulled me from under the coop when a chicken snake wrapped itself around my neck and I froze and could not move. I had no conscious memory of the incident, but the experience was buried in my subconscious, leaving me with nightmares of hundreds of snakes crawling over me on the bed at night. A few years later, Mom casually mentioned the chicken coop incident at Grandpa's farm which helped me understand my overwhelming fear of snakes.

My mother was a stay-at-home mom who never left us with a babysitter. She took us everywhere with her. Subsequently, during the first five years of my life, I was never separated from my mother except for church and visits to my grandparents. Whenever Mom called my name, "Patricia Lynn," in that distinctive "I-mean-it-this-time" tone of voice, I intently hung onto every word she spoke.

When my mother walked me into my first day of kindergarten class, she failed to mention the plan included leaving me at school. Therefore, I was completely shocked to see my mother quietly leaving the back door of the classroom. The teacher physically grabbed and held my arms from behind to prevent me from running after Mom, now out of sight in the hallway. I was furious - how dare she lay hands on me, only my parents had the right to physically touch me. I twisted out of her hold on my arms, turned around to face her, and kicked her on the leg as hard as a five-year old can - having three siblings to wrestle with turned out to be a tremendous asset; then I victoriously ran out of the classroom to my mother. Mom was not happy; but apparently the teacher was even more displeased. I was thrown out of her classroom on the first day of kindergarten and assigned a different teacher the next day. After that, Mom ensured the three younger siblings were left with friends and relatives to prevent a repeat of the kindergarten classroom drama.

When Thumper, our pet rabbit, disappeared, Mom cooked dinner and placed a plate of "fried chicken" on the table. Upon announcing my certainty Thumper was on a plate on the dinner table, my siblings joined the rebellion.

Dad smoked non-filter Lucky Strike cigarettes from the age of fourteen and enjoyed his daily whiskey. At the age of sixty-five, Dad was diagnosed with lung cancer and given six months to live. I flew back for two months to care for Dad. He hated hospitals and insisted on staying at home, refusing any chemotherapy or pain medication.

It was unbearable to see the pain in his eyes. The doctor later gave me a pain medication patch to place in the middle of his back so he could not reach it and take it off.

The cancer had quickly invaded and devastated my dad's body. He lost over one hundred pounds during the two months I took care of him. He was now a six-foot, four-inch skeleton. When he fell in the bathroom one night, I found him on the floor with no clothes on, completely naked.

He calmly challenged me and laughed, stating, "Big bad cop, what are you going to do now?"

With confident resolve, my response was, "I'm going to get you up and get you in bed." I physically stood him up as he leaned on me for support and walked him to the bed.

Dad never lost his sense of humor throughout his struggle and to the end with this horrible disease.

I had to fly back home to check on the kids. I went in to work for a night shift when I received the call from the family. Dad was deteriorating fast and would not make it through the night. There were no available airplane flights leaving that night.

My sister later told me that he said, "Patty is here - she is always here when I need her." Devastating. This memory still overwhelms me. I was not able to get back there in time to be with him physically, but I was there in that room in spirit praying for him, comforting and holding him.

CHAPTER 4

Touched by the Hand of God

At eighteen years old, just out of high school, my first job was civil service administrative work at the army base at Fort Lewis, Washington. I married a Vietnam veteran who came home with PTSD after two tours in the war zone. At the time, there were no resources, awareness or understanding of PTSD and the danger of suicide. We were married for four months. It was destined for failure from the beginning.

Steve was severely depressed, drinking heavily, and physically abusive. One time, he deliberately drove the passenger side of the vehicle with me in the front seat passenger side and steered the vehicle passenger side vehicle body into a cement and steel bridge overpass railing suspended over fifty feet above a canyon. No-one was hurt, but the incident created fear and distrust. I attempted to seek counseling for him through his commanding officer at his current military assignment at Fort Lewis, Washington, with no proactive action taken at the base.

One evening after visiting my parents about a half hour away, I returned to our apartment. It was obvious he was extremely drunk and angry, wanting to fight. To avoid confrontation, I went into the bathroom and locked the door to take a shower. A few minutes later, the loud reverberating echo of a single rifle gunshot was heard from the adjacent bedroom about six feet away. In the recent days, he would hide behind closed doors in the apartment and jump out of hiding to grab and scare me. It was an overwhelming feeling of sheer terror – waiting for him to break in the bathroom door to kill me with the rifle.

My entire body was shaking uncontrollably, crouched in a fetal position kneeling on the shower floor. After a few minutes passed that felt like endless time passing, I managed to stand up and cautiously exit the shower, open the bathroom door, and peek into the bedroom. Not sure where he was located or where he was hiding now, I was positive that at any second he was going to jump out of his hiding place to place the rifle to my head and murder me. Inside that bedroom waited a gruesome indescribable scene - the smell of blood and gunpowder. The air in the bedroom was filled with a thick reddish mist of blood, small pieces of brain matter, and bone fragments. His now lifeless body was not immediately visible, lying face up on the carpet floor between the far side of the bed and the closet wall with a rifle lying on top of his body.

Police investigators later determined he had placed the rifle under his chin and pulled the trigger one time to ensure suicide. Several neighbors in the apartment complex called the police. I was now hysterical, in a complete state of shock, unable to stop shaking. The officers responded, and my parents were later notified and came to the scene. During their at-scene investigation, the police officers located several empty bottles of vodka and beer in the kitchen garbage can.

My parents drove me back to their home after the police released me. My father, a man I had never seen cry before my entire life, broke down sobbing. It was late at night. I was by myself in the back seat of the car with Dad and Mom in the front seat.

A flood of sadness, grief, fear and horror overwhelmed me. Senseless. He was so young, only 19 years old. *Why didn't he kill me first?*

My mind plunged and fragmented, filled with incomprehensible grief. Then in a singular moment in time I experienced a genuine life- changing miracle, sitting alone in the back seat of the car in the darkness. Suddenly and unexpectedly, I felt the distinctive pressure of a hand on my right shoulder from behind me. Simultaneously, at the same moment, I was enveloped and flooded with a sense of a higher power that instantly replaced my horror and grief with a sense of absolute, unconditional, undeniable peace.

God was riding in that back seat with me that night. I had not prayed or asked God for help, feeling he was much too busy taking care of others throughout the world that needed his attention. I was completely wrong. My all-knowing Creator and his angels were there with his grace and eternal love during the darkest moments of desperation of my young life.

God, a higher power, or one of his Angels sent from above, took away the grief and despair and instantly replaced it with peace and grace - more powerful than anything I had ever experienced before in my young life. The experience was completely unexpected and undeniable. To this day, it is still impossible to capture and describe in words - *surreal, supernatural, not of this earth.*

I then fell into a deep sleep with no memory of walking into the house and sleeping in my parents' bed. My next memory was waking up the next morning with the grief and pain engulfing me again. However, I now possessed absolute confidence in God's power and grace, with his angels watching over and protecting me. God's eternal love and peace were waiting for me in heaven.

During this experience, and for over forty years later, I did not talk about this, even with my family; at the time I was young in 1972, just turning 19 yours old, and felt the experience would be unbelievable to others. Later as a police officer with LAPD our policy did not allow voicing personal opinions about religion, politics, social current events or personal beliefs with other officers and civilian staff, or the public.

Heaven is filled with incredible love, peace, light, and God's angels. No wonder people describing near-death experiences are torn about staying in heaven's pure light and love, or going back to their children, family and unfinished things waiting back on earth.

I was touched by the hand of God in those moments, fully engulfed with his undeniable love and presence. From the moment I was born, God had a plan and a path for me from the moment of birth. It was a Calling to join the Los Angeles Police Department - God guided and protected me. God sends guardian angels to watch over every one of our first responders in the military, law enforcement, fire, and medical paramedics and doctors serving in the line of duty.

There are no coincidences.

CHAPTER 5

Recruitment, Academy Training, Probation

Multiple factors influenced my decision to join the Department. My second spouse had joined the Department first. He would come home and tell stories about his daily shift work. I listened and realized I could do the job and probably do it better!

The physical test in the police academy included a six-foot wall, a one-and-a-quarter mile hill run in under ten minutes, and two pull-ups on a chin-up bar. The biggest challenge was the pull-ups. Females do not have natural ability for upper body strength to pull up their body weight on a bar. My first attempt was a complete failure, unable to pull my body weight up even halfway. A pull-up bar was installed in the hallway entryway between the living room and hallway at my home. Every time I passed through the entryway, I hung onto the bar with my body weight and tried to do just one pull-up. Miraculously, after two solid weeks of attempts, a successful perfect pull-up was attained. Over two months, fifteen pull-ups eventually followed.

Prior to starting my academy class training, I followed a personal intense running program of three to five miles, five days a week. I also had a fitness program working with weights at a local gym. A few months into the academy training, the class instructors appointed me as 'head road guard' during our daily academy class runs on the streets surrounding the academy; I developed a passion for running that lasted the remainder of my career. I trained and participated in several Department sponsored annual Baker to Vegas law enforcement international 120-mile "Baker to Vegas" relay team runs, with each team consisting of twenty team members. Each team member ran approximately six plus miles in the relay run over a race on roads consisting of desert afternoon heat over 110 degrees and part of the race up a 5,500-elevation mountain at night, usually with high winds and infrequent snow blizzards.

Throughout my career, I relied on physical fitness and jogging for stress relief. Future training programs also stressed physical and mental fitness for officer survival and to maintain a 'position of advantage' at all times during suspect field contacts.

While in the academy, I had a seven-year old boy and a five-year old girl. Spending as much time with them as possible was a priority, balanced with the demands of the academy hours and rigid training program. I practiced my handcuffing and arrest and control techniques with the children, which they loved, although they sometimes reported the handcuffs hurt their wrists. Both children loved the play wrestling and the "suspect-get-away" scenarios. This game consisted of taking turns playing the suspect and the officer, with the designated suspect trying to escape the wrist locks and handcuffing, ending in a play foot pursuit of the suspect on the front lawn.

One morning, my daughter asked me to stay home, "just this one day." I did not have an option to take the day off because of the academy rules - new recruits were not allowed to take any extra days off during the six-month academy, except for sickness or death!

To this day, I deeply regret not placing my child as a priority over the academy that morning.

One night, upon arriving home from the academy, I was surprised to discover roof shingles from the house scattered everywhere on the lawn in the backyard. Upon questioning, my seven-year-old son innocently responded, "The babysitter helped me get on the roof to play flying saucers with the shingles." Needless to say, that person was immediately replaced the same evening.

The arrest and control portion of the academy involved a one-on-one designated recruit as the "suspect" with a designated recruit field officer. Under the class instructor's close supervision and scrutiny, the recruits were directed to take away the officer's holstered .38 Smith and Wesson four-inch revolver. The recruits were not issued or allowed any live ammunition except for the shooting range; all guns are inspected and clear of any live ammunition prior to the practice.

My mind was already made up that no one would *ever* take away my weapon under any circumstances, even during practice training. Every officer should utilize officer survival tactics and training in practice, which is instinctively relied on in the field under stress - all officers react instinctively in the field the same way they practice in training. Giving up my weapon meant death and was not an option.

The instructor ordered the recruit "suspects" to take away the recruit officers' guns. I was the designated officer and quickly covered my gun grip and holster with both hands and dropped to the ground on my right side, using my body to protect the gun. The instructor focused on the recruit assigned with me as he struggled unsuccessfully for over four minutes to remove my gun. Impatiently, the instructor stood over the recruit "suspect" and stated, "Recruit [name], what is your problem? Get her gun *now*."

The stressed recruit was still unable to obtain possession of my holstered gun. Finally, the instructor directed the recruit to get my side handle baton attached to a ring on my gun belt on the exposed left side of my body. The recruit "suspect" easily removed and retrieved my baton. I quickly stood up, unholstered my gun, took a shooting stance, and ordered the recruit to drop my baton or he would be dead - ending the scenario. This mental mind set was critical in real life for officer survival on the streets in Chapter 9.

Four years later, I came home after an officer involved shooting incident, emotionally exhausted, only to discover my spouse, without discussing with me, told both children about the shooting incident before I arrived home. Consequently, my daughter refused to go on a planned school class tour of the downtown Los Angeles Children's Museum the next day. As a parent, I was furious with my husband. My daughter adamantly stated, "There are bad people in the city that will try to hurt me." Upon reassuring her and attending the trip with her and the class, she finally agreed to go on the trip. I had not realized how deeply my work impacted my children until that powerful moment.

There is an inherent pride in wearing the badge and uniform and upholding the Los Angeles Police Department's great tradition and history of honor and integrity. Legendary leader Los Angeles Police Chief Darryl Gates, well known for supporting all the officers, led our Department at a time where city politics did not interplay with basic leadership concepts derived from military models.

CHAPTER 6

Welcome to Foothill Area

My first patrol assignment was at Foothill Area in the San Fernando Valley, an area labeled affectionately "The Rock," covering Tujunga, Sunland, and Sun Valley. Foothill Area was one of the geographically largest areas of the city. At the time, there were eighteen geographic LAPD divisions in the city.

In 1983, the black-and-white police vehicle light bars replaced two round 'Mickey Mouse ears' sitting on the roof of the car. Portable mobile radios called "rovers" also came a little later so the field officers could carry the rover on their gun belt outside of the vehicle. The radios were also affixed in front of the middle console of the vehicle dashboard, along with a computer (MDT) on a swivel between the driver and passenger seat.

Foothill had a reputation for having some of the most senior field training officers (FTOs) in the city. I was brand-new, out of the academy, and eager to learn field police work. Working the morning watch shift, our watch commander was very gruff, and anyone who called in sick was called a "weak suck whiner!"

My first FTO at Foothill Area stated that I was not aggressive enough in the field. Taken by surprise, I thought I was being respectful while learning the nuances of field police work. Later the same day, we went in pursuit of a motorcycle rider refusing to pull over for a traffic violation. It was common for motorcycle riders to evade the police, and this violator was no exception to the rule. As the passenger officer, I broadcast our unit was "in pursuit of a motorcycle, [location] and direction of travel, requesting an additional unit and an air unit."

A few minutes later, the motorcyclist crashed into a tree of a residence. A Code Six (at scene and location) was broadcast as I ran over to the suspect, now lying on the grass. I was determined to get to the suspect before my partner. I handcuffed and searched the suspect, requested an ambulance, then broadcast a Code Four (suspect in custody) then stated without emotion to the FTO, "Was that satisfactory enough for you?"

While on probation, the first backup call at Foothill Area was an officer needs assistance request for a "Code Tom," a fifty-thousand volt taser, for an aggressive combative suspect. The primary unit had already deployed a Taser on this suspect, with no effect. Upon arrival at the scene, we observed a Hells Angels biker suspect. He was muscular, powerful with massive biceps, and weighed over three hundred pounds. The suspect was combative with the officers already at the scene, and the first Taser deployed had not affected him. PCP is a hallucinogenic known to cause violent and unpredictable behavior in which the drug user does not feel normal pain, such as with broken bones. Reports were documented of subjects breaking their wrists without feeling any pain to get the handcuffs off.

Positioning myself about six feet from the suspect, I ordered him to get his hands up or the Taser would be used. The suspect ignored these commands. I held the Taser Unit Control as it discharged with approximately ten feet of two separate thin wire still attached to the two darts. The unit made a distinctive, methodical, repeated clicking sound to verify with the user that the unit was activated, working properly, and fully charged. The two darts were separated and attached to the suspect's clothing on his upper chest.

The next events were shocking and surreal - The suspect laughed causally as he pulled out the two darts and held a dart in each hand in front of his massive chest. The taser had no obvious effect on him except to become more aggressive and combative. The electricity arched and glowed between the two darts held in his upraised hands. The fifty thousand volts of electricity arching in a distinctive dancing chalky white rainbow of electricity between the suspect's hands was eerily illuminated behind a canvass backdrop of night darkness.

The suspect then stated to all the officers at scene, "I'm going to kill all you motherfuckers now." Every one of the officers at the scene believed him.

The suspect threw an officer over the hood of a nearby police vehicle. One officer was able to strike the suspect in the stomach with his baton, leaving the suspect with the wind knocked out of him for a moment. The suspect fell to his knees.

Although afraid, I was a female on probation. Death was preferable than showing any fear. Moving to the suspect's right arm, I was absolutely amazed to be able to place his gigantic arm behind his back for the handcuffing process. Other officers jumped in at the same time to handcuff the suspect's arms behind his back. It took three sets of handcuffs to complete the handcuffing process due to the size of the suspect.

Remember in 1983, most male officers had not embraced working with female partners in the field. Some officers held preconceived negative opinions about females on the job. Females could not hold their own if things went sideways in the field - right? I was determined to prove that females could handle field situations.

Welcome to Foothill Area!

CHAPTER 7

The Baby Boy and the Barricaded Door

Upon passing probation, Rampart Area was my next assignment. Rampart Area was the opposite of Foothill Area in regard to geographic Area with its small six-mile square size and easy to learn streets and directions. Rampart was a hardcore area to patrol with over fifty identified street gangs, including the infamous, now nationwide ruthless brutal Mara Salvatrucha "MS" gang, and the White Fence gang, oldest gang in the city. The 18th Street gang originated in Toberman Park, the south end of the division. In the early 1980s, Rampart led the city with murder and drive-by shootings. Gang, drug activity, and violence went hand in hand and were rampant. This assignment would last ten years and became the foundation for my officer survival and tactical skills and field knowledge. Broadcasting vehicle pursuits, setting up perimeters, handling drive-by gang shootings, and murder crime scenes became second nature.

On my first day working with John Vasquez, the tenured senior driver officer, I began typing license plates of Toyotas and Hondas on the mobile digital terminal (MDT) computer keyboard. Rampart had over three hundred reported stolen Toyotas and Hondas every month. A possible reported stolen vehicle was soon identified. This information was immediately related to John.

His response, "Are you sure?" At the time, there were very few females in field assignments. The comment surprised me.

My response was, "Yes, pretty [explicative] sure," while aiming the MDT on the front middle dash swivel into his right knee for emphasis.

John then turned the vehicle around to catch the two suspect occupants going in the opposite direction. The stolen vehicle with two juvenile occupants were detained and arrested without further incident.

We talked about it afterward. John related the prior day he worked with a female officer. She told him a vehicle was reported stolen. After the stop, they determined the vehicle was a reported "lost or missing" license plate, not a stolen vehicle. We both laughed about his experience that had occurred the prior day.

John and I were assigned together a few months later when we received a Code Three radio call with multiple persons reporting (PRs), "Shots fired in progress, second-floor apartment." Due to the multiple PRs, we knew it was a good call with a possible active shooter.

Two other units also responded to back us. The neighbors were contacted and reported that the husband and wife, with their nine-month old baby boy lived in the apartment. Several gunshots had been reported fired inside the residence prior to our arrival. An entry team plan was made. John and I were the assigned primary unit on the call, and we would enter through the front door first.

However, when one of the officers attempted to kick the front door to allow entry, we discovered the door had a heavy piece of furniture barricaded across it on the inside, preventing entry more than about six inches. My partner, John Vasquez and I both felt an extreme sense of urgency due to the several neighbors reporting multiple shots fired with a baby and his parents inside the apartment.

I stated to my partner, "I think I can get inside the door if I take off my gun belt," thinking if I could gain entry, I could possibly move the object barricading the door from the inside.

John responded without hesitation, "You are not going inside without me." This powerful moment is one of the most treasured moment that solidified our bond, trust and partnership forever.

We both took off our gun belts and, with our primary weapons in hand, we entered through the small door space together - John squeezed through and "button hooked" to the right and I "button hooked" to the left. John covered the hallway and rooms to his right while I cleared my area of responsibility - the kitchen, isle countertop, and dining room area. After clearing and securing the initial front entry kitchen and dining area, we were able to focus on moving the massive solid wood dresser that barricaded the front door to allow our backup partners to gain entry.

We quickly retrieved our gun belts and gear. The remainder of the apartment was cleared room by room down a long hallway. At the end of the hallway, one room with a closed door remained to be cleared. During the entire entry and search and rescue efforts inside the apartment, we never heard a sound from the family calling for help, or the baby crying. Approaching the last bedroom door with everything eerily quiet inside the room, I was engulfed with an inescapable feeling of overwhelming dread.

Inside, a male and female adult lay on the bed, both face up. Each of them had a single gunshot to the head; both were deceased. The baby was lying frozen with eyes wide open, in a pool of blood between his deceased parents. Miraculously, he was alive and uninjured. My all-encompassing instinct was to get this baby out of this hideous scene.

Holstering my gun, I instinctively picked up and embraced that baby boy covered in blood, in my arms. He was held close to my heart over my uniform shirt, badge, and vest to comfort him as he was carried out of this room of horrors.

Years later, my partner, John Vasquez told me the day we rescued the baby behind the barricaded door with multiple shots fired, *"I did not need a vest - I had you."* This was another moment that captures the undeniable essence of the powerful bond between true partners entering the unknown danger waiting for us on the other side of that doorway. We never had to question each other's tactics and movement - with genuine blind trust and instincts between two partners entrusting each other with our lives.

Three years later, while responding on a routine radio call, the female person reporting (PR) mentioned she had not had contact with police since her sister was killed by the husband in a murder and suicide. This woman was now raising her nephew, the only survivor of the incident. The boy was not present at the home. I had a flashback to that moment when I picked up the baby and embraced him in my arms. I was overwhelmed with shock and emotion; but did not want to upset her.

I was only able to speak three words without showing any emotion to her, and stated calmly, "I was there."

She related that her nephew was a happy child, and he was doing well. A framed picture of the boy was on the living room shelf.

God placed me at the scene for a reason, and it was meant to be for me to later meet the boy's guardian for a reason. It gave me comfort and relief to know this little boy was safe in a loving home.

There are no coincidences.

CHAPTER 8

Multiple Shots Fired

Another emergency call in Rampart Division: "Shots fired, possible multiple victims, Code Three." There were multiple persons reporting, shots fired, in progress. My partner, Mike, was the driving officer. Additional information was reported of a running gun battle with the suspect, husband killing his wife's boyfriend, then chasing and shooting his wife. As we approached the location, the suspect was observed outside the apartment complex in front of our police vehicle. The suspect held a handgun in his right hand hanging at his side.

Mike parked the police vehicle facing the suspect approximately seventy feet away from him in the parking lot of the apartment complex. The suspect stiffly and slowly turned to face us, standing without saying any words. His facial expression was emotionless. He appeared to be unresponsive and in shock, unable to express any pain or feeling.

Mike and I positioned ourselves behind the open police vehicle doors. Mike gave the suspect orders to drop the gun and get his hands up. Suddenly a little boy, approximately eight years old, came running up behind me. The boy was panicked and hysterical, running directly toward the suspect with the gun.

Stating to Mike, "Cover me," my complete attention focused now on the safety of the boy. Leaving cover of the vehicle door, I wrapped my arms around the boy to move him out of the dangerous line of fire, while using my upper body and vest to protect him. The boy frantically began twisting around and pulled out of his tee shirt to get away. He was a tenacious little guy, intent on escaping my arms to run toward the suspect.

During this struggle, the suspect suddenly raised the gun to his head and killed himself with a single shot. The boy was inconsolable.

Tragically, the investigation revealed the suspect was the boy's father. This turned out to be a three-way love triangle in which the suspect killed the boyfriend with the gun, then shot the boy's mother as she tried to escape out of the apartment. She later survived her gunshot injury. The suspect then shot himself in front of that little boy, who was trying desperately to get to his father. There is no way of knowing if this desperate father would have shot his son before killing himself given the opportunity. My heart was broken for this young child who had just witnessed his father committing suicide in front of him.

CHAPTER 9

The Michelin Tire Man

During the start of day watch shift, I was working an L-car (one officer unit) on a corner of a business district with heavy going to work traffic, standing in a parking lot. Suddenly, approximately fifteen panicked people ran on foot down the sidewalk toward my position, yelling and screaming for help.

Immediately I observed a huge male suspect over six feet tall and heavyset who resembled the "Michelin Tire Man," a male about six feet tall with what appeared to be layers of round tires encircling his body under his XXX large size tee shirt. It was almost comical; the suspect growled and snarled as he chased the group of people from a distance of about fifty feet behind them. As a coup de grace, the suspect prominently held a forty-ounce full beer bottle in his right hand.

The crowd of frightened people, now huddled together on the opposite corner of the busy intersection, watched intently as I assessed the situation and stepped between Mr. Growly and the crowd.

In my firmest command presence voice, I ordered the suspect repeatedly to drop the beer bottle. The suspect ignored my commands, instead raising the beer bottle over his head in a threatening manner.

In a somewhat unorthodox and risky move, I swung my side handle baton one time aiming at the suspect's right hand and glass beer bottle.

The suspect could possibly use large pieces of the glass to assault me if this plan did not work. The baton struck the suspect's hand and shattered the glass beer bottle. The suspect immediately deflated like a helium balloon, becoming dejected and docile from the shock of the bottle shattering in his hand.

The crowd, still watching intently from the other street corners, shouted and cheered in excitement. The suspect was taken into custody without further incident and transported for a mental evaluation hold as a possible danger to himself or others.

I was relieved the suspect gave up and no one was hurt.

CHAPTER 10

Officer Needs Help

Most officers have a moment in time where their training and mental officer survival skills are tested. They develop an inherent "heightened awareness" to constantly read their surroundings. All good cops instinctively watch and read body language and mannerisms of their field contacts. This provides a better "position of advantage" to react to the suspect's actions. Physical and mental officer survival is ingrained in us to "Fight back no matter what and never, never give up."

Every day while driving to calls for service, I mentally rehearsed 'What if' scenarios:

What would I do if a suspect attacked me, refusing orders to stop and get his hands up and try to physically overwhelm me? At what point would my weapon be drawn and lethal force be required?

My moment in time occurred in 1987, working Rampart Division as an L-car (one officer unit) while my partner was in court. I was assigned a residential theft incident in which a family reported a tenant stealing their property. The PR provided the suspect's name and description, as well as his local hangout, MacArthur Park. While scouting the park for the suspect, I observed a possible suspect on foot in the crosswalk at Park View Avenue and 7th Street. Positioning the police vehicle front and engine block between the suspect and myself,

I stood behind the open driver side door for cover. The suspect was asked, "What is your name?" He immediately stopped and focused solely on my position with a crazed look, clenched teeth, and foam coming out of his mouth. I knew at that moment he was intent on rushing and overwhelming me.

From approximately thirty feet away, the suspect rushed toward my position behind the parked police vehicle open driver door. I focused onto the suspect's left hand in his front left pants pocket, which contained a large distinctive bulge. I repeated over and over to myself, "Gun or knife, gun or knife," as the suspect refused my repeated orders to "Stop - get your hands up."

Based on the totality of my observations and the suspect's behavior and actions, I was convinced the bulging object in his left front pocket meant imminent "death." The suspect continued to rush toward my position behind the open vehicle driver's side door as he ran around the front of the parked police vehicle, clearly intending to overwhelm and take my weapon which I held in my right hand. However, the suspect's weapon in his left front pants pocket was not yet visible to me. The Department's deadly force policy and training emphasizes deadly force is to be used as a last option. I chose to wait as long as safely possible behind the vehicle driver side door.

I relied on my training, focused primarily on gun retention due to the threat and the suspect's intention to overpower me and take my gun to kill me. Holding my six-inch Smith & Wesson revolver in my right hand, I turned the right side of my body away from the suspect and raised my free left arm up and close to my body to protect my gun hand. Approximately five feet from the open driver vehicle door, the suspect pulled out a huge buck knife and simultaneously attempted to stab the right side of my body in the same motion. Four shots were fired with my gun still held in my right hand, focused on his left hand and arm holding the knife - the immediate danger. I later learned the suspect was left-handed. The suspect, now in shock from gunshot injuries, walked to the back of the police vehicle and sat on the curb. I reloaded my gun first, then initiated a "shots fired, officer needs help" broadcast. Every on duty Rampart unit responded to the help call.

The investigators later determined the suspect had a prior arrest record for assaulting a California Highway Patrol motor officer. The suspect rushed and "sucker punched" the officer in the face. He then pushed the officer's motorcycle over on top of him. Backup officers observed the officer on the ground with the suspect on top of the officer attempting to take the officer's holstered gun. Apparently, this suspect had issues with authority figures.

During attendance of numerous officer survival training classes, I had never practiced one-handed close contact shooting. I later practiced one-handed shooting specifically for gun retention. You fall back on your training and officer survival skills in these life and death incidents. The remainder of my career, I also carried a backup two-inch revolver around my ankle and switched my primary weapon to a Beretta 9 mm semi-automatic with three magazines.

Research shows officers fighting for their lives become angry and think about their family. In my case, I became enraged that this suspect was trying to take me from my children. Afterward it is also common to later play the scene over and over in your mind like a tape recorder. During the incident, the gunshot rounds traveled in slow motion and no sound of gunfire was heard. To this day, I have a distinct feeling of panic when surrounded by crowds or strangers and avoid crowds.

CHAPTER 11

Catching the Bad Guys

The first black-and-white photo below, aged five, I was holding two toy pistols - "I'll get the bad guys!"

The second black-and-white photo below, when John Vasquez was six years old with his little four-year-old sister, Mary, playing cops and robbers - "I'll get the bad guys!"

We were born for law enforcement work, guided by God's plan to help others, instilled with a deep calling to protect the vulnerable and the innocent, and to make a difference. Without any hesitation, we would die for a total stranger.

In later years, John Vasquez, my partner, proved to be an advocate, mentor, and a proactive leader for LAPD female officers on the job. As the first male Vice President of the Los Angeles Women Police Officers and Associates (LAWPOA), he influenced positive change for countless females on the job. He coordinated and planned the LAWPOA annual Women's Leadership Conference for several years. I am deeply honored and proud to work in the field as true partners with John, who entered through that door with me, not knowing if we were going to meet a dangerous suspect with a gun that day of the multiple shots fired behind that barricaded apartment door.

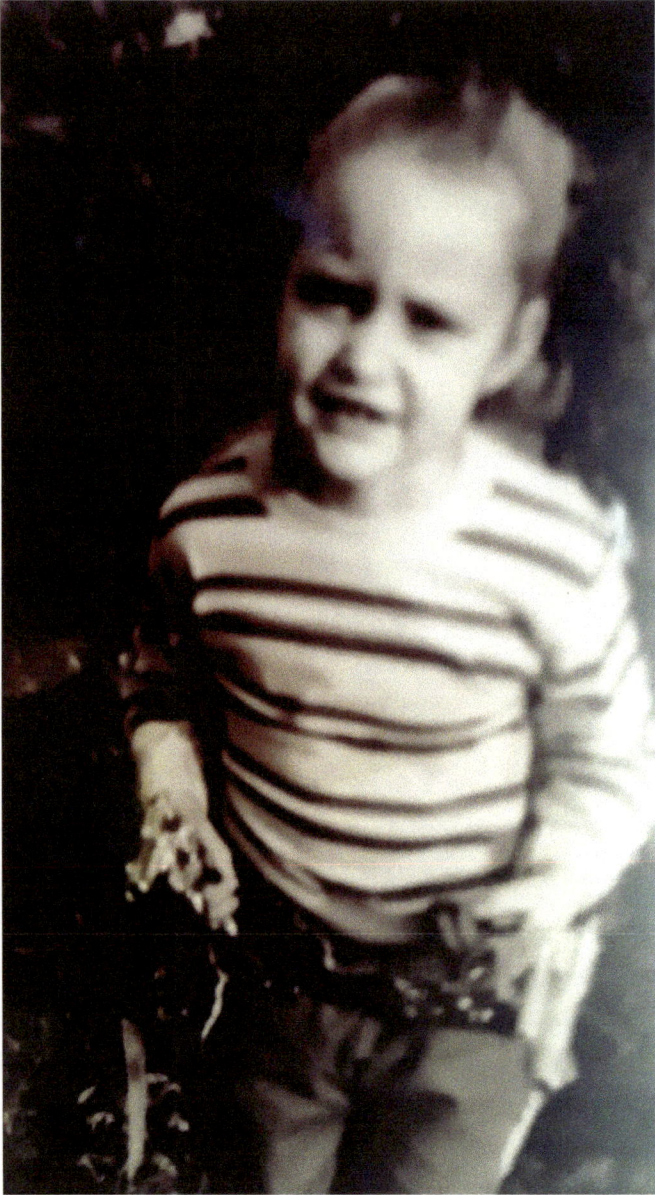

"Catching the bad guys"

"Catching the bad guys"

West Valley Parolee Unit
"Catching the bad guys"
(See Chapter 15)

One day, while working a day watch plain clothes narcotics assignment in Rampart Division, I was positioned on a public sidewalk, corner of a business, waiting for a radio signal for a hand-to-hand drug sale. Just around the corner of the building, a female suddenly screamed for help. Taking a quick peak around the corner, I observed an elderly woman struggling with a male suspect to keep her purse. The suspect pulled the woman to the ground and started running on the sidewalk toward my position, with the woman's purse in hand. I had the advantage of surprise with the suspect not recognizing me as a police officer. As the suspect ran past where I stood, I stepped onto the sidewalk. I used my leg to trip the suspect and my right forearm to push the suspect forward while using his momentum to propel him forward. The surprised suspect landed face-first on the sidewalk and was quickly handcuffed. It is highly unusual for an officer to witness and interrupt a purse snatch in progress. The crime was interrupted, a felony suspect apprehended, and a frightened elderly victim got her property back - all with no injury to anyone, including the suspect, the victim, or officers.

There are no coincidences.

A few days later, I transported a narcotics arrestee to the main downtown jail at Parker Center in the early-morning hours. The long hallway corridor stretching approximately 150 feet long on the bottom floor was completely empty and quiet with only dull yellow hue overhead ceiling lights. As I escorted a handcuffed arrestee toward an empty room for an interview and examination for possible under the influence of narcotics, our voices echoed as the suspect asked a question.

Suddenly I heard loud noises and voices around the far corridor hallway. A handcuffed suspect turned the corner at the far end of the corridor at full run, with a single police officer following behind. him.

Even handcuffed people can run almost full speed. The suspect ran directly toward where I stood, holding one arm of my arrestee with my left hand. I moved the arrestee close to the wall for the arrestee's safety.

As the suspect neared my position, I stepped closer and tripped him, simultaneously using my right forearm to push him forward (a proven technique from the prior field purse-snatch arrest). The handcuffed suspect's momentum and the slippery tile floor resulted in the suspect sliding on his stomach and body like a snow sled on a steep, downhill snowy mountain, about twenty feet down the hallway. The officer was then able to regain control of his uninjured suspect and stood him up on his feet. The officer meekly whispered a "Thank you" to me as he escorted the suspect away.

While working another undercover narcotics incident, I was working follow-up clues and reports of narcotics activity at the Cameo Hotel, a location well known in the area for narcotics sales. My partner and I were conducting a narcotics complaint at a third story apartment. I was standing outside the apartment in the third floor hallway with the suspect in custody for a minor narcotic charge at the location while my partner secured and locked the apartment. Suddenly, a male stepped outside the adjacent apartment. Upon recognizing my narcotics undercover dark-blue jacket with the word 'police' in large block white letters, he immediately turned and ran down the length of the hallway. The corridor ended with a window three stories high, with no outside balcony, railing, or stairs, and no other way to exit.

This individual aroused my interest due to the generally accepted law enforcement rule that innocent persons normally do not run away when they observe police officers. I calmly escorted the suspect in custody to the second suspect's location at the window to ask him some questions regarding his actions. Upon attempting to engage this suspect in conversation, he completely shocked me by jumping out the three-story window, falling onto the ground below. I looked out the open window, expecting this person to be lying on the ground, injured and unable to move. Instead, I observed this suspect bounce up and continued running up the street without any apparent injury. It was obvious this person wanted to get away from the police more than I was inclined to jump out the same window. Additionally, I had a detained suspect in custody. The suspect was probably on some kind of drugs, and he did not feel any pain. Any police officer who tried to jump out the window after him would have likely been severely injured or paralyzed!

The next day, my partner and I returned to the hotel's third floor and contacted several neighbors. They advised this person had felony warrants and did not want to go back to jail. Warrants issued by the courts stay in the system until the subject is detained and taken to court. An automated computer want-and-warrant (AWWS) query during the suspect's next future detention would identify the warrant - it was just a matter of time.

CHAPTER 12

Mentors and Leaders

Lieutenant John Desmond was a Rampart night watch commander who mentored and encouraged me to apply for a Field Training Officer (FTO) position. In 1987, the position of FTO was held by mostly male officers. Along with myself, there was only one other female FTO at Rampart. The position of FTO is critical to instill the Department's mission "To Protect and to Serve" and to reinforce our Department core values with new probationers.

Lieutenant Desmond assigned me a few of the most problematic probationers. One of them, first name of Hector (fictional name), was new out of the academy. Remedial training was soon recommended for report writing and officer safety issues for tactics and not knowing our unit location.

Officer safety, officer survival, and field tactics were an ongoing focus. Officers should always know their location and cross streets to respond quickly. This could be challenging dependent on the graphic area covered, added with nighttime shift work and lack of familiarity with the division. The division maps issued became essential along with clues such as north/west streets were odd address numbers, and south/east even numbers. Another valuable tool of police work is memorization of all the streets in progressive order. This enables the officer to visualize the quickest driving route for a Code Three emergency high priority call or "officer needs help" broadcast.

This new probationer was struggling with the basics of police work. He never knew his location and demonstrated weak field tactics. He was brought in for meetings with the watch commander several times during the next week to develop a positive remediation learning and training program.

During an ADW suspect with a knife radio call, we responded to the scene. Hector was designated contact officer. As he approached the suspect's position, Hector placed his baton directly in front of the suspect while he conducted a pat down search and handcuffed the suspect. As guarding officer, I immediately moved the baton away from the suspect's reach with my foot, an officer safety issue.

After the suspect was placed in the police vehicle for transport, Hector was asked, "Why did you place your baton in front of the suspect? You gave him your weapon."

His response, "That is what we were taught in the academy." Wrong answer.

The second meeting with Lieutenant Desmond occurred when I parked my private vehicle in the station parking lot. Hector was off duty and appeared disheveled.

He approached my vehicle, stood next to my open driver's side window and stated coldly, "Now I know what vehicle you drive to get even." Wrong statement.

My response, "Get into the watch commander's office right now."

Daily training documentation was mandated for all probationers' progress. Hector was reportedly observed by other officers to be literally crying tears in the male locker room about his training officer assignment with me. He hated my documentation on his progress.

After the second incident, I recommended that the probationer be assigned with a new field training officer to gain some fresh insight and ideas to assist this probationer with his training progress. Lieutenant Desmond's response, "Give it one more shift."

The next shift, Hector was the driver officer of the police vehicle. As we responded back to the station, Hector turned in the wrong direction and headed onto some side streets. While approaching a stop sign, Hector speeded up as we approached a posted intersection stop sign.

I verbally and adamantly ordered him, "Slow down - stop sign, stop sign!!"

He then deliberately sped up and drove through the stop sign as he adamantly replied, "Document that, Officer Gerst! [my married name at the time]" At this moment, I was convinced he was capable of watching me bleed out slowly on the streets of Rampart from gunshot wounds without calling for help.

He was ordered to pull the police vehicle over. I drove back to the police station. After the meeting with Lieutenant Desmond, the probationer opted to resign. Not everyone is cut out to become a police officer.

With Lieutenant Desmond's encouragement, I later applied and became the first female Senior Lead Officer (SLO) responsible for community relations in Rampart Division.

The value of working with the community members left a lasting imprint. One of my successful quality of life community projects was written up and published in the universally recognized Police Executive Research Forum (PERF), a well-known national police research magazine.

Lieutenant Desmond later encouraged me to apply for the sergeant's test. This resulted in promotion and transfer to Wilshire Division. Lieutenant John Desmond has passed away. He was a rare extraordinary mentor and leader who truly made a difference within the community and with the officers he supervised.

Upon promotion to sergeant, I was transferred to Wilshire Division and later tasked with forming a "handpicked" Special Problems Unit (SPU) due to the gang and narcotics street activity. One incident resulted in an officer ambush on the part of a local gang member. The community was terrorized and intimidated by this out-of-control gang activity. The gang members typically broke into local resident apartments and homes to hide from the police. The residents were terrorized into silence with the fear of gang retaliation.

One of the first actions implemented was to set up a dedicated "1-800 Tip Hotline," where the area community members could anonymously call and leave crime tips. Every community tip was followed up on and investigated.

Due to the violent gangs on the streets, the SPU team members were directed never to chase a suspect; instead, they were directed to set up perimeters and requested the air unit and K-9 dogs to safely search for the suspects.

During one incident, two team members chased a suspect wanted for narcotics possession. The officers quickly set up a perimeter around a large apartment complex. While at the scene, I received a call from the watch commander with a citizen report of a gang member hiding at the rear of the apartment building with a gun. The air unit and K-9 dog teams were already responding. The air unit and K-9 dog and handler assisted with apprehending the suspect and recovered the loaded gun without further incident and without injury to the community members, suspect, or the police officers.

My next assignment was Van Nuys area, where I was a field sergeant, and later appointed as the gang OIC. During routine monitor and gang intelligence gathering in a well-known local gang area, I discovered a frightened female pit bull with the letters "Blythe St." written in red felt marker across her head and down her neck and back. A group of boys were hanging out nearby. Upon inquiry of the dog's ownership, the group advised the dog was a stray. The dog was transported to the station, and animal control was notified. Later, a Van Nuys officer adopted this abused orphan. The new owner reported about a year later this dog was the sweetest and most loyal dog he had ever owned. This dog and the officer had found each other, safe and this turned out to be her loving safe place in her "forever home."

CHAPTER 13

The Baby Girl and the Monster

Witnessing pure evil is the most challenging part of the job. Our purpose is to fight evil. Tragically, sometimes we fail.

As a sergeant supervisor, I was assigned a possible child abuse station call to Children's Hospital where a little four-year old girl lay on a hospital bed in a coma. She was a beautiful thin fragile child with long black hair, weighing no more than fifty pounds, hooked up to breathing tubes, not moving, eyes closed - in a coma. Interview with the treating doctor determined this baby girl had "shaking baby" trauma and suffered ongoing physical, sexual, and emotional abuse.

Physical examination of this tiny child and follow-up investigation identified bruises covering every inch of her body, from the suspect poking her over and over while forcing her to run in circles on top of the kitchen table. She sustained the "shaking baby" trauma from being thrown against a wall and showed evidence of old injuries with broken bones in various stages of healing. This suspect drove the child around in his vehicle for over an hour, waiting for her to die before taking her to Los Angeles Children's Hospital that night.

The child's mother was holding a one-year old baby girl during a meeting at the hospital waiting room. The mother denied her husband ever harmed her child in any way. My response, "Not only did he hurt your little girl, but he is also going to do the same to that baby you are holding when she gets older."

Later interviews of the child's grandmother revealed the child had sought help by telling her grandmother about the abuse. This mother immediately isolated the child, preventing her from seeing her grandmother again.

Follow-up investigation at the home revealed evidence her father had sodomized the child and used a turkey baster to remove the semen. The coroner's office autopsy later identified extensive layers of bruising in the child's anal area. This innocent child died during the night at the hospital.

This evidence was presented in the court trial. The monster in the darkness will never again be able to hurt this precious child, this baby girl with long black hair who never had a chance. In my heart forever - she will never be forgotten. This child's torture and the ongoing cruelty and every form of abuse was haunting.

I could have requested a police unit to take over the investigation but really did not want more officers to be haunted by the emotional side of this horrible scene. We all had children at home. I maintained my professionalism, ensuring the proper notifications were made and evidence was secured for court trial.

Standing face-to-face and looking directly into this suspect's cruel cold eyes - I had looked into the eyes of pure evil.

Pure Evil does exist.
Monsters in the darkness do exist.

CHAPTER 14

Fugitive with a Gun

It was a quiet Friday on the detective floor. Unfortunately, my Special Problems Unit (SPU) on the floor was off duty on days off. A few days prior, my special problems team had responded to assist with a domestic violence call in West Valley Area, with a female victim reporting her violent boyfriend as an out-of-state felony attempt murder fugitive from the state of Nevada. The suspect possessed a handgun, and his location was unknown to the victim at the time of the investigation. The victim had a three-year-old son living with her.

In police work, there is a saying, "Follow the girlfriend to catch the bad guy." Since a few days had passed, there was a high probability the suspect had gotten back together and made up with his girlfriend. I gathered the intelligence background case file and crime flyers with the suspect's photo and checked out an undercover vehicle. I then set up on the female's parked vehicle in the back parking lot of the apartment complex early in the morning. About an hour later, she entered her vehicle with her child. They were followed to a nearby moving rental company. The male suspect was not present.

While the female was inside the rental office, I called the station and requested an officer to assist with the contact stop. As she got into the front seat of a rental van, the responding officer and I made contact in the rental company parking lot. I advised the female she was endangering her child and harboring a dangerous fugitive with a gun. During the interview, the female confessed the plan to assist the suspect to leave the area and she confirmed the suspect had a gun. The suspect was reportedly waiting at a local motel notorious for narcotics and prostitution activity. The female was planning to pick the suspect up outside the front of the motel at noon.

The officer was directed to take the female and her child to the station while the Van Nuys Division watch commander was notified of the suspect's location. I set up a command post in a large business parking lot a block from the motel.

I had to stay at the command post to run the operation. A frequency was requested to be reserved so that regular radio field transmissions would not interfere with our communication. The backup units were briefed on the armed and dangerous fugitive and given the crime bulletin flyer with the fugitive's photo. A sergeant was assigned with the officers on the perimeter to contain the outside of the motel. An air unit was requested to stay in the area near the location.

At noon, an officer on the perimeter broadcast the suspect standing outside in front of the motel. He looked around then reentered the building.

A few minutes later, another officer on the perimeter broadcast the suspect exiting the rear of the building. The air unit was called in as four officers moved in to surround the suspect. The officers observed this fugitive holding a gun in his hand. As the officers surrounded the suspect, he was ordered multiple times to "Stop, drop the gun, get your hands up."

The suspect disregarded the orders as he turned to confront the officers while raising the gun toward them. Upon seeing he was surrounded by numerous officers with the air unit overhead, the suspect decided to surrender and drop the gun.

The officers who apprehended the fugitive had a rush of adrenalin. They were elated to catch the armed and dangerous fugitive that almost ended in a shooting situation.

At the command post, I had called the air unit to the location, listening intently to the radio broadcast reporting the officers confronting the armed suspect - feeling helpless and fearing for those officers' safety. I silently prayed for those officers, waiting breathlessly. It felt like hours for the radio broadcast, "Code Four, suspect in custody" - and an overwhelming rush of relief when the radio broadcast confirmed the suspect was safely in custody without further incident.

As a leader in a dangerous fluid situation, my demeanor was consistent, calm, and deliberate during this dangerous and fluid incident to reassure and give the at-scene officers confidence. Prayers of silent thanks were sent to God and his guardian angels for watching over us that day.

CHAPTER 15

The ATM Robbery Suspect

One of my old supervisors at Rampart Division reached out and offered an administrative assignment as a researcher at Management Services Division. I was working a Van Nuys Division gang unit at the time. It is never wise to say "No, thanks" to a commander, and I highly respected Commander Daniel Koenig's integrity and leadership. It was also an opportunity to further develop writing and investigative skills as a researcher and internal affairs investigator. I also had the opportunity to attend the Department's supervisory intense four-month-long West Point Leadership Course.

Upon promotion to lieutenant, I was assigned to West Valley Area as a watch commander. During roll calls, I wanted to provide recent crime information and review Department policy and procedures. It was also important for the officers' morale and to have some fun. There was always an end of watch (EOW) Code Seven question used from various sources in police history, LAPD policy, and the History and Discovery Channel. One time I forgot to ask the question and dismissed the roll call with the words, "Be safe out there." Everyone sat and waited. I asked what was wrong. They were waiting for their EOW Code Seven (lunch break) question.

Quickly I asked, "What gets better gas mileage, a truck with the tailgate up or down?"

The officer who won answered, "With the tailgate down due to the air flowing more efficiently."

Later I was assigned to the detective floor and supervised a parolee team. The team trained together in undercover surveillance operations, building entries, and search warrant service.

On the detective floor, we continuously analyzed crime patterns. One crime pattern identified was a local drive-up ATM. The suspect would approach the victims' parked vehicle after the money was withdrawn, demand the money with a gun, and escape on foot in daytime hours. This method of operation (MO) was repeated five times in two weeks.

The parolee team drew up a surveillance plan focused on the safe capture of the ATM suspect. Rusty and Andy were hard-charging energetic partners, a perfect team for undercover work. Undercover partners were set up along with chase vehicles' offset to be directed in by radio to catch the suspect.

The parolee team and the separate special problems team on the floor took turns covering the target location. We switched off every day for continuous coverage. Officers are competitive by nature, and the two teams already competed for the highest crime arrest and clearance at West Valley. My team's productivity was consistently higher compared to the other team.

A few days later, the other team was embarrassed to be set up on the targeted location and somehow missed the robbery go down at the location. Long-term surveillance work is tedious and brutal over a period of hours, much less days.

My detective commanding officer partner wanted to cancel the entire operation due to resource demands, but I was insistent in continuing the undercover surveillance operation.

Two more days into the daytime operation, our parolee team was set up on the target location. Being very "hands on" as the OIC of every specialized unit assignment, I worked side by side with the unit members and thrived on safety, intelligence gathering, tactical planning, briefing, and training of every operation. I was usually the radio officer and provided supervision over the operation. The team members were deployed in the surrounding area around the target location. I was with Rusty and Andy in an unmarked vehicle, parked across the street in a parking lot. We then observed a male matching the description of the suspect, tall thin White male with a black hoodie in the middle of the day in one-hundred-degree weather, walking toward the ATM location.

As the radio officer, I notified the undercover and black-and-white chase vehicle officers set up and waiting in black-and-white vehicles in the area, "It's going down right now," with the suspect's description and location. The air unit was requested to the location. I was a huge fan of using the air unit helicopter and the k-9 dogs as a resource.

Andy Taylor immediately exited the vehicle on foot to "keep eyes" on the suspect. We moved in as the suspect approached and attempted to rob a victim in a vehicle at the ATM drive-up. As we moved in, the suspect fled on foot down a back alley next to the ATM and attempted to hide in a large dumpster. Andy was close enough to the suspect to follow him. The suspect was contained and arrested without further incident.

A rollback and search warrant service to the suspect's location was conducted to gather more evidence for court prosecution and to recover any stolen property to return to the right owners.

Outstanding police work!

Rusty Redican, our parolee unit team member and his partner, Andy Taylor, exemplified our calling to be police officers and to serve the community. Rusty was tenacious and dedicated but also extremely charismatic and outspoken. Rusty requested the below incident be mentioned in reference to the teamwork, planning, and training which was put in place for every parolee check and warrant service. Every warrant and every incident was fluid and required escalation or de-escalation dependent upon the suspect's actions.

At the time, Assembly Bill 109 was passed by California legislation, impacting enforcement of parolees. Our parolee team focused on conditions of parole and/or sex registration to ensure accurate reporting of newly released parolee addresses, job status, and other information. At the time of release, all parolees and sex registrants were given clear and specific conditions for contacts with the police. Parolees who did not comply with officers' directions could also have their parole revoked.

Our unit responded to a sex registrant's address to verify the address and other records. The team set up on the location. One of the team members knocked loudly on the front door and identified himself, stating, "Police officers, open the door." The subject looked through the window next to the door and observed four officers wearing police undercover jackets with insignia identifying them as police in large white block letters. The subject had no doubt officers were at the location to talk with him. The residence had not been cleared, and other occupants could be inside the residence destroying evidence or arming themselves with a weapon.

Instead of opening the front door, the subject shouted, "Who are you looking for!"

After the third time of the officer repeating the order and the suspect refusing to open the door, I stepped up to the porch between the door and window for the subject to clearly see me and stated to him, "It is the [explicative] police, and you know it is the police. We are here to talk with you, so open the [explicative] door right now." Then the subject was reminded he was violating his parole conditions. The subject immediately opened the door, and the officers were able to verify the parolee's information without further incident. Sometimes you have to speak the suspect's language in order to de-escalate the situation.

CHAPTER 16

Courage and Leadership Under Fire

My courage and integrity were tested at the end of my career, but not from outside on the streets - the adversity came from within the Department. Internal politics flourished within the Department. At West Valley Division, my detective commanding officer partner had never worked as a watch commander or OIC of a specialized unit team. He held some animosity towards me for not recruiting him into a Van Nuys gang unit that I supervised as the OIC. This golden boy came from the Chief's back office. His leadership style differed dramatically from my leadership style. Leading up to the ATM undercover operation, he deliberately encouraged conflict and division on the floor, pitting my parole team of seasoned patrol officers against the detective team assigned to him.

Unfortunately, the conflict and jealousy harbored between the two detective teams exploded after the ATM robbery suspect was arrested. A fielding briefing was held to serve a search warrant and roll back to the ATM suspect's residence. Both specialized teams were present. During a field briefing for a search warrant service and rollback to the ATM suspect's residence, the robbery table detective supervisor openly committed an act of conduct unbecoming an officer. The detective stood in front of Andy and coldly stated, "You should have been shot one more time in your shooting and died," as he chest-butted Andy. I immediately stepped in between the detective and Andy, ordering the detective to stand down. Of course, Andy's partner, Rusty, exploded in rage as he was extremely protective of his partner. They had worked together for several years, and Andy had almost died in an on duty-shooting incident. This detective's statement and actions were disgusting and shocking and clear serious misconduct. Rusty and Andy were directed to respond back to the station to separate the two teams.

As a witness to serious misconduct on the detective supervisor's part, I demanded a formal complaint be filed for investigation. This never happened. Conversely, allegations of misconduct were filed against Rusty and Andy. Their complaint allegations were sustained and later overturned.

Standing up against this injustice, I was very vocal. Once you stand up against the system, you become a target. Soon the Detective CO came into my private office and closed the door. He wanted me to order Rusty not to come on the detective floor.

My immediate response: "That is an illegal order as the officer has a locker on the second floor, and I will not give this officer an illegal order."

The detective CO was furious. He was obviously testing me as he had the power to give the order directly to the officer himself.

Because I stood up for the two officers on my team and was very vocal, I was removed from the detective floor without an assignment, packing my documents into boxes and carried them downstairs. I had worked closely with a truly knowledgeable professional staff person, Spence Leafdale at West Valley Division. I asked him if I could store my two boxes in his administrative office on the first floor.

Spence rescued me and offered an assignment to work administrative duties investigating, interviewing, and final adjudication of formal investigative complaints against officers, called letter of transmittal (LOT). Spence had been subjected to unfair treatment in the past by his supervisors. He had a strong understanding and insight into the Department complaint disciplinary system. He had fought back hard for his reputation, and justice prevailed in his case.

Trained to fight back, I reported the situation to the Valley Bureau. Meetings were held with Valley Bureau command staff. This resulted in a transfer to Foothill Division, the same division where my probation was completed in 1983.

CHAPTER 17

Cavalry Mounted Unit

My new Foothill partner was Detective CO partner Kristine Kenney. We possessed the same leadership and supervisory style - "*Do the right thing and treat each other with respect.*"

Kris, like me, came on the job in the early 1980s and rose through the ranks the hard way with competence, professionalism, and an "old school" approach. During personnel briefings, we would finish sentences with the exact same words. Assignment on the Foothill detective floor was rewarding and challenging.

Area Commanding Officer Sean Malinowski was a visionary Area CO. He developed and implemented a *'predictive policing'* team to interrupt, disrupt, and disperse criminal activity. This system used a crime statistical algorithm crime data dump over several years to predict the day of the week, time of day, and location of criminal activity to provide extra patrol during that M.O . and time period to interrupt and prevent the activity.

Over the next three years, Foothill Area was Number One of the 21 Areas citywide for crime reduction citywide - beating its own crime statistics each year. At Foothill, hundreds of potential crimes and crime victims were reduced and prevented for three years, 2012, 2013, and

2014, particularly with property crimes - theft, residential and business burglary, carjackings and street robberies.

Detective Adjutant, Andrea Sansone, had extensive experience as a tenured civilian supervisor in overseeing and handling critical radio calls at Communications Division, along with the demands from bureau for projects on the administrative side. She was tenacious, diligent, a tremendous asset.

Captain Malinowski tasked me with forming a unique volunteer horse and rider mounted unit, now called the Valley Community Cavalry Rough Riders (VCCRR), under the supervision of LAPD personnel to "observe and report" criminal and nuisance activities by providing high visibility, crime prevention, and public outreach to establish a partnership and trust with the community. Teddy Roosevelt's volunteer group was historically the first horse-and-rider volunteer group in our nation, originally called the Cavalry "Rough Riders." Most of the children lived in poverty and had never touched a horse in their life. The children were ecstatic with the interaction in a safe environment.

Our Cavalry mission statement emphasized safety, professionalism, team building, horsemanship skills, and training. During our quarterly training days on horseback, the unit trained together with a focus on the mission statement. The instructor, or team leader, called the horses and riders into "story time," in a circle around the instructor, to ensure all the riders were able to hear the training or briefing directions. This technique was learned during a week-long training with my personal horse, Mocha Latte, at an Annual California State Mounted Police Officers Association (CPOA) Training Program in Northern California.

Prior to deploying the Cavalry horses-and-rider team in the field, all my field experience and tactical knowledge was relied on as well as horsemanship skills and understanding horse behavior. Formal uniforms with patches and name tags were designed. The horses and riders were required to attend ongoing training and evaluation tests to meet the formal mission statement goals for safety and minimizing risk management for the team members, horses, and the community members. The volunteer team members were expected to be familiar with LAPD Department policies and our new VCCRR formal manual.

During the extensive training days, the team members and sworn officers attended field scenarios to reinforce the importance for the volunteers to never engage in nuisance or suspicious activity in field deployments and to report the activity to the nearest at-scene sworn officer. These volunteers work and interact closely with assigned sworn police officers at every field deployment or event. Over ten years later, this unique Cavalry team, with over twenty volunteers and horses, are currently active today with a record of no injury or safety issues to the community or the horses and riders.

Crime patterns were monitored on a daily basis on the detective floor. The crime analysis detail isolated a pattern of a male and female suspect stealing baby formula in enormous quantities from a local Target business with a large parking lot. These two suspects also targeted several other Target businesses in the local San Fernando Valley and Santa Clarita area. The predicted day of week and time of day was identified for the location. It was a perfect detail for the cavalry riders.

Three horses and riders were deployed in the business parking lot before the predicted crime would take place. Within minutes, the two suspects were apprehended, and a roll back to the suspects residence was conducted to recover any evidence and additional stolen property with a warrant.

CHAPTER 18

Where Are the Real Leaders?

Ultimately, Kris Kenny was targeted by a few detectives on the floor when they disagreed with her leadership style. These disgruntled detectives collaborated and generated false complaint allegations against Kris, who was suddenly and arbitrarily removed from the division by a bureau commander (based on a one-sided conversation with one of the disgruntled employees) and assigned to a Valley Bureau office assignment.

Outspoken again, I made my support for Kris clear to the Valley Bureau commander. Kris was one of the strongest leaders I had ever had the honor to work with. Not surprisingly, I was targeted by the command staff and not supported. The Department is random and arbitrary in the handling of personnel disciplinary complaint issues. The same disgruntled detectives then generated several false complaint allegations against me and several other detective supervisors. They were empowered and emboldened by Kris's unfair and unjust removal from her command.

The working environment on the Foothill detective floor, once extremely productive, was now dysfunctional and ineffective. The Department Valley Bureau command staff chose to support the few disgruntled detectives without proper formal interviews or investigation, resulting in several lawsuits against the city.

True leaders put the best interests of their personnel before themselves. True leaders provide guidance, direction, encouragement, mentoring, proper training, and the support and resources to complete their assignment safely. Sworn officers require a strong relationship of trust and support with their command staff, direct supervisors, as well as their local community members. The officers' morale and confidence is directly impacted by their supervisors and leadership. In turn, the officers can provide their community members with the highest quality service possible.

Throughout the nation, law enforcement officers have been crucified by false stereotypes perpetuated by the media and a small group of biased individuals with "cop hating" and 'defund the police' political driven agendas.

Each officer involved lethal force shooting case is unique and should be reviewed and analyzed fairly on its own merit based the facts and evidence gathered from the incident, the officer's knowledge of the situation at the time, the officer's actions and tactics, risk management and the specific department's training, lethal force policy and procedures. It is essential to recruit, train, and retain quality and qualified personnel to be an effective law enforcement agency.

CHAPTER 19

Crime Victims and Emotional Devastation

On the Foothill detective floor, the investigations for crimes are the responsibility of the table detectives, dependent on the crime category. Each detective has a caseload which focuses on documentation of the case status, gathering evidence, interviewing witnesses, recovering stolen property, and serving search warrants as needed. These cases are then presented to the District Attorney's Office for prosecution. The most violent and heinous crimes involve murder cases.

One homicide case involved a victim, approximately twenty years old, who lived in a local project area known for drug and gang activity. Sadly, this girl became involved in prostitution, a very high-risk activity particularly in an extremely dangerous area of the division. The girl was found deceased in the early morning hours in a dirty parking lot near a trash dumpster. The Foothill homicide detective team and the on-call detective supervisor responded to the murder crime scene.

As time passed, no progress was made in solving this case. The victim's mother requested a meeting at the station with the assigned detectives. I attended this meeting. The meeting was held in the detective CO private office on the floor.

The mother stared directly at the assigned case detective and repeatedly asked, "How do you know this is my daughter? Are you sure?"

The detective hesitated, then finally responded, "Yes, from the tattoos on her body."

The victim's mother was sitting on a chair next to me. Upon hearing these words, this mother collapsed, sobbing inconsolably, filled with unimaginable grief, and threw herself onto my lap. My heart was broken for this person. I whispered to her over and over and over, "I am so sorry," embraced and held her, and rocked her in my arms like a baby.

The depth of a parent's love is forever and never- ending. No words exist to erase the overwhelming pain of losing your child, taken in such a senseless, violent manner, with no closure of suspect apprehension and prosecution for a senseless brutal murder.

Yes, sadly, there are a significantly small number of improperly trained, incompetent, uncaring officers throughout the nation the come on the job and show up for work for all the wrong reasons and bring disgrace to the public image of all law enforcement officers. The majority of our men and women in blue are human beings, with emotions and compassion for others, and want to make a difference. During chaos and heartbreak, we stand steadfastly to fight against evil and the monsters in the dark.

CONCLUSION

Police work has a powerful human and emotional side. Everyone must have the courage to choose to stand up and fight against evil to conquer and defeat it.

When I shared my spiritual experience forty years later with a coworker, Andrea Sansone, she pointed out, "God also calls on us (as first responders) to be guardian angels and warriors to fight against evil forces in the world." Imagine the powerful significance of making a difference and touching the life of even one person in their time of desperation and need. Reflection upon my life brings undeniable realization that God has been present, guiding and directing me. God called on me to watch over, train, mentor, and provide leadership to all the personnel I have had the honor to work with side by side.

After more than forty years after my life-changing experience, God has called on me to share my childhood's life-changing miracle with others. Our Creator sends guardian angels to comfort, watch over, and to protect us in our greatest time of despair and need. Hopefully, these words of comfort and hope will make a difference in even one person's life.

Evil comes in many forms and shapes to deceive and defeat God's hope, love, and peace. Recognize the beauty and promise of hope in simple daily miracles, such as a covey of quail crossing in front of your path, hummingbirds hovering at lightning speed nearby, a pair of red-tail hawks soaring overhead in the air, and a colorful sunrise of rich red, blue, pink and yellow. Also, recognize the powerful miracles that touch and change your life forever, such as holding a newborn baby in your arms for the first time.

Never forget the courage of our men and women in blue who proudly and steadfastly put on the Kevlar vest, gun belt, and place their lives on the line to protect total strangers on a daily basis. God sends guardian angels to surround, shield, and protect them.

Never forget our courageous sisters in blue, trailblazers who came before us and shattered false glass barriers for us to follow. True strength of character, leadership, and courage are reflected during times of adversity, not in easy times. Recognizing the right thing to do and doing the right thing are separate, and doing the right thing is always the hardest and most difficult choice to make. And sometimes you have to stand up with courage to ensure that others do the right thing.

Those who choose to be silent in the face of corruption accept corruption. Stand up with courage against corruption, deception, violence, and untruths. Silence means acceptance.

Theodore Roosevelt stated, *"No man who is corrupt, or who condones corruption of others, can possibly do his duty by the community." Secrecy and silence are the key to their power."*

Douglas MacArthur stated, *"A true leader has the confidence to stand alone, the courage to make tough decisions, and the compassion to listen to the needs of others. He does not set out to be a leader but becomes one by the equality of his actions and the integrity of his intent."*

Colin Powell stated, *"Leadership is solving problems. The day soldiers stop bringing you their problems is the day you have stopped leading them. They have either lost confidence that you can help or concluded you do not care. Either case is a failure of leadership."*

My favorite leadership quote is by Winston Churchill, "*Without courage, all other virtues become meaningless.*"

God has a plan and a calling for each of us, but he also allows us to have free will to choose our own destiny.

By God's design, there are no coincidences.

VCCRR INDEX/PHOTOS

The VCCRR photos that follow depict the community children's pure joy of touching a horse for the very first time for most of them.

Photo One and **Photo Two** are VCCRR team photos during the annual Chatsworth parade. The planning, training, and preparation for a color guard and parade of this nature is intense. Each entry is individually judged, and our team is proud to be awarded Equestrian Entry title four years in a row.

Photo Three and **Photo Four** taken in South Central Watts Projects. I will never forget this little boy who stayed with the pony all afternoon during a Christmas Day toy giveaway. Felicia, team member, is handling the pony, Lacy. There was something about hugging the pony that touched his heart. It was incredibly moving to all the cavalry members at the scene. This child did not wait in line for his toy, instead staying with the pony. At the end of the day, I had to tell the boy that Lacy was tired and needed to go home. The child walked with Lacy to the parked horse trailers. This boy said goodbye to Lacy just before she was loaded into the trailer. In **Photo Four** at the same event, Felicia is handling Lacy while Blake interacts with a community member in a wheelchair with his dog and pony Lacy –in a FULL CIRCLE of interaction, a special and shared moment.

Photo Five is a photo of a Christmas Chatsworth equestrian parade event, where our unit later won first prize in the judging of our equestrian unit. During our field mounted unit deployments, all the children loved touching the horses in a safe environment, usually with ground support nearby. Mocha was always gentle and loved the interaction with the small children. Some of the children had never had the opportunity to touch a horse before.

Photo Six is in a business center in Foothill Division. I asked this woman if she wanted to pet Mocha Latte. She stated her concern that the wheelchair would scare the horse. Laughing, I reassured her Mocha would love to say hello. Mocha and I were trained by the California State Police Officers Mounted Association, and he was completely bomb-proof around children and other distractions. This woman was delighted, beaming, and laughed out loud when Mocha put his head on her lap.

Photo One and Photo Two

Photo Three and Photo Four

Photo Five

Photo Six

DEDICATED TO MOCHA LATTE'S LEGACY

B ased on several events experienced throughout my life, I possess an undeniable realization that our Lord has a plan and path for each of us from the moment of birth. The below is a life lesson of the meaning of true loss and grief, strength and the courage to overcome adversity.

This personal testimony is dedicated to my amazing special gift sent by God - Mocha Latte. The following personal photos and special song lyrics are dedicated to Mocha's incredible story of incredible special bond between a horse and a person - a legacy of a true angel warrior horse. He was in a herd of about twenty-five horses in Castaic, California. I was not looking for another horse, helping a friend pick up a horse to take to her house.

Mocha was young, and for some reason focused on me standing on the other side of the fencing. He came up deliberately and stood in front of me, staring at me with his kind gentle brown eyes. When he reached over the fence and nuzzled me in my arms, I asked the rancher, *'What's his story?'* The rancher replied that he was born and raised for cow cutting, and the horse failed miserably at that job. This beautiful young brave horse stood in front of me and would not leave.

Of course, this horse ended up in my horse trailer, and taken home that same day. I did not know at that time what an incredible extraordinary horse our Father from above had sent to me – a cherished treasure.

Based on his color, he was called the rarest unique color of all breeds, a "gruella" - Dark grey with a rich thick black mane and tail, a black dorsal stripe running from the top of his shoulders to his hind quarters ending at the top of his tail, black leggings with a touch of white and a perfect white blaze on the front of his face - markings similar to the more recognized buckskin horse markings. This boy was named "Mocha Latte" based on his color and gentle attitude.

After spending time riding and getting to know him, I realized he was "green broke" to ride, but incredibly willing, gentle, intelligent and focused on what I asked from him. We quickly bonded and trusted each other. Please note in every photo of Mocha when I am riding him, he has his ears turned back towards me. He is listening to see what stupid thing I am going to ask of him - but never once refused!!

I had just been assigned as the Officer in Charge of a unique volunteer mounted Cavalry unit at Foothill Division by Area Commanding Officer Sean Malinowski. This Area had the vast isolated trails and parks of Hansen Damn in San Fernando Valley. Access into the park for patrol was problematic, traditionally requiring 4 X 4 motorized all terrain carts or Valley Traffic officers with off road motorcycles. Our new mounted horse unit was an ideal resource for this rugged terrain, as well as high visibility presence in local business mall parking lots for crime prevention.

Mocha loved the training days with the other horses. He had an easy-going disposition and confidence, which was ideal for training with the other unit horses. He was a bright student, and quickly learned to side pass, back up carefully around the cones set up on the ground that if knocked over were major points lost - the cones were *'pretend children'* in public situations! He also weaved through the spitting noisy red fire flare patterns with ease, showing the other horses not to be afraid. He was soon relied on to demonstrate to the other horses to complete the training obstacles with confidence. Horses are "predator driven" by nature. I instructed the unit and took the photo of the horses having fun chasing the police vehicle with the light bar activated, rather than panicking and running away in field situations. Later I circulated the photo at Foothill Division to include the patrol officers to submit slogan for the photo. The proud winner was given a certificate for lunch at a local restaurant. The winning slogan chosen was, *"FOOTHILL, Where No Pursuit is Normal."*

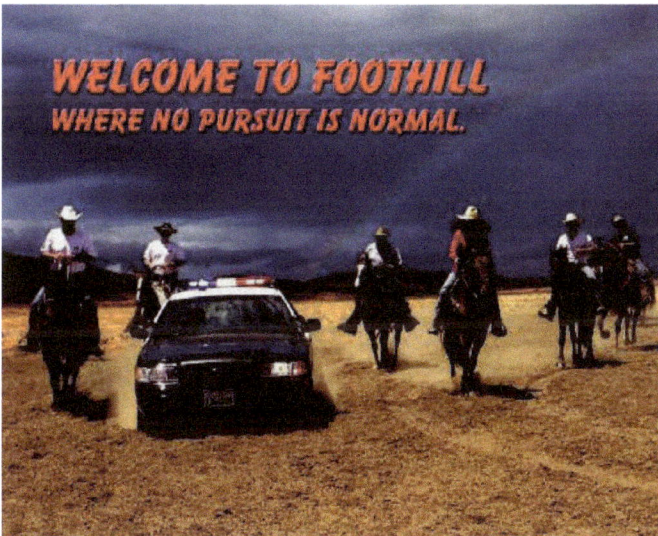

Helicopters hovering overhead and landing on the police station roof helicopter pads during field situations become a normal work day. Mocha carried me through thunder and fire.

Mocha and I had the honor of acceptance to attend an intense weeklong mounted horse training course with the California Police

Officers Association. I was incredibly proud when Mocha easily passed all the obstacles, including through water, backing, side passing, single and column of two movement with other horses side by side. I was thrilled, particularly when Mocha won the "battle ball" soccer game, kicking the huge three-foot-high plastic blow-up ball over the goal without hesitation - with our two-man team winning the competition!! He later never wavered in the face of a crowd of pretend protesters waving flags, raising their arms in the air and shouting in front of him.

My greatest test with Mocha came unexpectedly during a test at night in a huge covered show arena with 75 horses. We were in columns of twos with Mocha and I approximately twenty horses from the front, along the outer barn building metal wall. The instructors had let us know to be prepared for fireworks to be set off to simulate gunfire. When the fireworks were ignited, the horses in the front immediately panicked. Chaos broke out as I observed the horses in the front rearing up and twisting sideways in a domino effect backwards towards our position - feeding off of the fireworks explosive sound and sparklers shooting into the air. I instinctively reacted with calmness, relaxing in the saddle, and deliberately loosened the reins to reassure Mocha and give him his head - trusting him to choose the best escape from the trap along the inside wall and the hysterical horses throwing themselves into each other. Mocha stoically and quickly moved sideways as he picked the best avenue of escape to safety away from the panicked horses throwing themselves into each other. Amazingly, Mocha got us out of the danger to safety in the open area on the inside open area of the arena. Looking around the completely chaotic scene, several riders ended up on the ground with the possibility of being stepped on, with several frantic panicked riderless horses running loose around the arena. Fortunately, only one rider went to the hospital with a broken pelvis and no horses were severely injured. Mocha's calm actions saved us from injury in a critical dangerous situation, definitive proof of our special trust and bond!!

Mocha and I later conducted countless deployments in the field as part of outreach into the community outreach to interact with children, most who had never touched a horse before. We also participated in color guard flag presentation. Our color guard detail honored celebrated over 75 young teens and adults in the grandstands receiving U. S. Citizenship.

At Foothill Division, a crime pattern was identified throughout the local area, with a male and female suspect entering a local chain of stores that sold baby formula. These two suspects were involved in the burglary of thousands of dollars of the stolen merchandise. The suspects' description and photos from store cameras, method of operation (MO), time of day, and day of week were analyzed and identified. A plan was drawn up based on analysis of the data. Uniform officers were offset, and our mounted horses deployed in the area of the store based on the projected pattern. These two suspects were apprehended within ten minutes of the predicted time for the crime to occur, a roll back search warrant conducted, and items of stolen property were recovered along with evidence to be used for court purposes. Mocha patiently waited and moved in when the operation went down. The suspects were apprehended in the act without injury to the suspects, our officers, the store personnel, or the horses and riders.

During a huge public ride with a council member in Chatsworth, San Fernando Valley, we were riding near three LAPD mounted unit horse and riders leading the group in the front. The LAPD horses suddenly stopped and refused to go down a steep embankment with a stream of water on the bottom. I respectfully and quietly asked if Mocha could go first, knowing Mocha would calmly go through the water. Sure enough, without hesitation Mocha confidently showed the other horses how to drop down the bank and go through the water. The other horses quietly followed Mocha. I was absolutely proud of my trusting horse that day!!

I had the habit of taking sunrise and sunset photos; and one day I saw the opportunity to snap a unique stunning photo of Mocha standing in a backdrop of an incredible beautiful sunset of rich colors of red, orange and yellow, and rolling gentle hills. After completion of the book, this photo was used for the design of the bookmarks and business cards.

Mocha quickly schooled me on his favorite snackies – The round peppermint treats from the restaurants were preferred over apples, carrots, pears and grapes. Anytime I drove home or talked to him, Mocha always came up to me searching my pockets for the treats. Mocha thought the other horses and rescue burro were a nuisance, and always preferred special attention and face rubs from me. Mocha taught me the meaning of courage, strength, love and grace under fire.

I had Mocha for almost 20 years before his sudden and unexpected death from a possible heart attack - words cannot describe my broken heart. Mocha was my partner; we had a special unspoken trust and bond. Mocha, my angel warrior horse now protects me from above, and spreads his wings over the earth in the shining light of every sunset and sunrise.

The narrative summary of the book promised several suspenseful surprises in store for the reader. Therefore, in addition to Mocha Latte's legacy and special story, this conclusion ends with song lyrics in the form of a poem written in memory of Mocha Latte and his extraordinary legacy; along with a second theme song written for the sacrifice of all our brave First Responder warriors and heroes. These two special song lyrics are from my heart, and they are in the process of musical production soon to be available on my website for readers to enjoy and contemplate:

Warriors and Heroes.com
Touched by the hand of God Send Me.com

YOU CHOSE ME

Mocha Latte Lyrics

In a herd of horses
You were brave and young
You came to me and nuzzled into my arms
You would not leave
You chose me forever
We shared a special bond and trust
You looked at me

You would not leave
OUR FATHER FROM ABOVE SENT YOU TO ME
YOU CHOSE ME!

I took you into my life
You became my life
I CHOSE YOU FOREVER
WE CHOSE EACH OTHER

A special bond and trust
We watched over and protected each other
You carried me through thunder and fire
Mocha, Mocha, Mocha

Saint Michael came
And called you too soon
So gentle, brave and valiant

Now you are overhead
Watching over me
Protecting me like you did before

TAKEN FROM MY LIFE TOO SOON
Angel horse with wings, warrior horse
Spread your wings over this earth now as you did

You are the shining light in every sunrise,
The shining light in every sunset
Whispers of you Mocha, Mocha

Angel horse with wings, warrior horse
Gentle, brave, and valiant
Whispers of you Mocha, Mocha
Angel horse with wings, warrior horse
You are deeply loved
hoofprints forever imprinted in my heart

Angel horse with wings, Warrior horse
Spread your wings over this earth now as you did
On the horizon as I sing this song to you
Mocha, Mocha, Mocha Latte

These words were written in memory, and special dedication to my horse, Mocha Latte - you are in my heart forever - never forgotten.

FIRST RESPONDERS THEME SONG

Called upon and sent by God from above
With a purpose from the moment of birth

Called to become warriors, protectors, rescuers
First Responders, heroes
Our Military soldiers, police, fire, and medical

To shield, protect and watch over us
In our darkest moments of despair, hopelessness and fear
In a battle of Good versus pure evil
To conquer pure evil and monsters in the dark

Called upon and sent by God from above
To Comfort, protect and seek justice
To comfort the innocent and the vulnerable
In their darkest time of need
To shine a light into the darkness and defeat pure evil

When the Lord calls upon them
These brave warriors, heroes
Stand up with courage, strength and faith
To defeat pure evil and the monsters in the dark

Shine a light into the darkness
Shine a light into the darkness–
Send Me
By God's design - There Are no Coincidences

ABOUT THE AUTHOR

Lieutenant I Patricia L. Blake, Los Angeles Police
Department 1983 – 2016

Patricia L. Blake was born in The Dalles, Oregon. She joined the Los Angeles Police Department (LAPD) in May of 1983, with over thirty-three years' experience upon her retirement in 2016.

Blake completed her probation at Foothill Division and was then assigned as a field patrol officer at Rampart Division, where she became one of the first two female Field Training Officers (FTOs) at Rampart. In 1987, Blake was recognized as the "Officer of the Year" at Rampart, and she was later chosen as the first female Senior Lead Officer (SLO) at Rampart Division.

As a sergeant, Blake transferred to Wilshire Division, where she developed a Special Problems Unit (SPU), targeting violent gang and narcotics activity. As the Officer-In-Charge (OIC) of this SPU unit, Blake and her special unit team received a Meritorious Unit Citation for impacting the quality of life in the local community.

Blake was assigned to Van Nuys Division as the assistant watch commander and was later assigned as the OIC of the elite Community Relations Against Street Hoodlums (CRASH) gang unit.

Blake was then called to work at Management Services Division as a Department researcher for the Chief of Police and Internal Affairs as an investigator.

Blake was promoted to lieutenant, where she was assigned to West Valley as a watch commander and assistant and acting detective Commanding Officer (CO) and supervised the West Valley parolee team. Blake then transferred to Foothill Division, where she was assigned acting and assistant detective CO and the OIC of the mounted horse and rider Cavalry unit (VCCRR). This unique unit provides outreach and 'good will' in the local community for crime prevention, education, and interaction with the children. The VCCRR responsibilities included search and rescue, park, dam and trail patrol, evacuation and emergency preparedness, high visibility theft and crime prevention in the mall parking lots, color guard presentation and parades. Upon retirement, Blake continued as a LAPD reserve officer OIC of the VCCRR unit for the next seven years.

Lieutenant Blake holds a bachelor's degree in criminology from California State University of Northridge, a master's degree from University of Phoenix in Organizational Leadership, as well as completion of the Department intensive West Point Leadership Course, and the Department Instructor Development Course. In 2016, she was recognized by the Los Angeles Women Police Officers and Associates (LAWPOA) for outstanding achievements, leadership, and mentoring contribution to the organization. Blake was affiliated with LAWPOA and the California Peace Officers Association (CPOA).

Lieutenant Blake has participated over ten times in the annual international law enforcement "Baker-to-Vegas"120-mile relay run sponsored by LAPD, with over 350 separate competitive law enforcement teams from our nation and throughout the world, such as Canada and Australia.

Milton Keynes UK
Ingram Content Group UK Ltd.
UKHW051033191124
451074UK00023B/32

9 798894 194950